Redeeming Advent

PURSUING CHRIST THROUGH THE HAZE OF TINSEL, GIFTWRAP AND LEBKUCHEN

LUCY RYCROFT

GILEAD
BOOKS
PUBLISHING

Gilead Books Publishing

www.GileadBooksPublishing.com

First published in Great Britain October 2019

2 4 6 8 10 9 7 5 3 1

British Library Cataloguing-in-Publication Data:

A catalogue record for this book is available from the British Library.

ISBN: 978-1-9997224-8-7

Editor: David Burton

Cover design: Nathan Ward

Cover image ©Anna Tash

To my dad, Simon Baynes

The first writer I knew, and one of the best

Contents

Acknowledgements   6

Introduction   9

REDEEMING OUR HOME

Day 1: Advent as 'Coming Home'   13

Day 2: From Rags to Riches   18

Day 3: The 'Now and Not Yet' of Advent   24

Day 4: The Thrill of the Ride   30

Day 5: The Agony of the Ride   35

Day 6: Are You Prepared?   39

REDEEMING OUR CHRISTMAS

Day 7: What Are We Actually Celebrating?   45

Day 8: Can Anyone Tell What You're Celebrating?   50

Day 9: How Santa Can Draw Us to Christ   55

Day 10: Traditions and Surprises   60

Day 11: Joy to the World   65

Day 12: The Feast   70

REDEEMING OUR HEARTS

Day 13: A Perfectly Imperfect Advent 77

Day 14: The Advent Disaster 82

Day 15: A Cosmos-Sized Responsibility 88

Day 16: Stick to the Grid 94

Day 17: You Don't Always Get What You Want 99

Day 18: You Don't Always Get What You Deserve 105

REDEEMING OUR COMMUNITIES

Day 19: The Giving of an Unnecessary Gift 111

Day 20: When the Light of the World Feels
Insignificant 116

Day 21: Sweet Charity 120

Day 22: The Vicar's Kid at Christmas 124

Day 23: The Jobs Left Undone 130

Day 24: Cheerleaders 135

A Tail-Piece 140

Acknowledgements:

This is typically the section of a book where an author informs the reader of who they can blame for its creation. So, in no particular order, here are the guilty parties.

My blog readers - affectionately known as the Desert Tribe: your comments and responses are a constant source of inspiration and encouragement to me. If you weren't reading, I actually wouldn't be writing this now. You're enabling me to have a career I love. Thank you so much.

A handful of friends were particularly encouraging when I originally blogged these devotions in December 2017. Some even suggested that there might be a book in it. Colin Baynes, Derek and Marilyn Spicer, Francesca Shearcroft, Lesley Godson and Sarah MacBruithin - friends, it's time to come clean and accept some responsibility for the book you now hold in your hand. And thank you for being so kind. If you were just trying to make me feel better, well - surprise! It's led to an actual book.

Andy, Beth, Claire, Fiona, Jo, Liz, Sean, Tracy - thank you for such hugely kind words. Wow. I was tentative in sending my manuscript to the writers and leaders I most admire, but you humbled me in your gracious response.

Anna - what a beautiful cover. It's everything I wanted and more. Thank you for using your God-given talents to serve him and us.

Chris - thank you for taking a punt on me. I so appreciate your experience, wisdom and considered oversight of this book. Thank you for putting everything together so well.

Dave - I'm so grateful for your editing, not least because I can blame you for any mistakes. But of course, there won't be any, because your thoughts on the manuscript were spot-on, and I'm so pleased to have been able to tap into your experience.

My children show little interest in anything I write, and for that I am hugely grateful. You guys are funny and kind and inspire me daily. Being your mum is one of the greatest privileges of my life. Thanks for unknowingly providing anecdote fodder.

Al, I don't know of any other marriage where such cutting sarcasm and deep respect exist side by side, but we've managed it for a fairly long time now. Thank you for taking God so seriously and yourself not so much. Thank you for constantly challenging us to live as radical disciples. I roll my eyes and tell you that you're being ridiculous, but it's all going in. And thanks for paying the bills so that I can pursue a pipe dream. One of these days you should read something I've written. Love you.

Lucy

York, 2019

Introduction

I am hopelessly lacking in spiritual discipline.

There you go. I've said it. By all means put this book back on the shelf and direct your hard-earned cash to another, better-deserving, more spiritual author instead. I promise not to hold it against you.

Or maybe you can relate to me, and that's why you've picked up my book. And I use the word 'my' deliberately. Not that it can't be yours too – in fact, I very much hope it will be, not least because every book you buy helps my son to squeeze another packet of Match Attax cards out of me – but this is *my* story, born out of my experiences during Advent, inspired by years of struggling to retain any sort of spiritual focus throughout December, and crafted one year for my blog because I didn't want to *yet again* lose Jesus through the haze of Christmas consumerism to which I always fall prey.

If this sounds like you, then welcome aboard – it's an absolute pleasure to be redeeming Advent alongside you. We will be focussing on Jesus, for sure, but through the window of all the other demands on our time and resources that appear during December. We will be shedding the guilt that we might feel about engaging with secular Christmas celebrations, and instead, using them as an opportunity for God to teach us and change us. I hope you find it relatable, helpful and thought-provoking.

The book is divided into four sections, each with six daily readings (but, hey, no one's going to tell you off if you skip some or get behind – make this book work for you). The first six readings will be about redeeming our home (reflecting that, when Christ comes again, we will go to our heavenly, true home), before we move on to redeeming our Christmas celebrations (how we can use our festivities to grow close to God), then to redeeming our hearts (dealing with a few of the less pleasant aspects of our character which can present themselves at this time of year), and finally redeeming our communities (looking at how God is calling us to interact with those around us).

If you wouldn't call yourself a Christian, well, hello! You are more than welcome. I'm guessing I don't need to tell you that I'll be writing from a Biblical perspective here, so you might need some sympathy for where I'm coming from, but that doesn't mean you need to agree with everything I say, of course. I hope you'll find plenty of shared philosophical territory in the Bible passages I've picked out – there is so much sense in the Bible, and I genuinely believe that those of all faiths and none can appreciate its wisdom. But I would be lying if I didn't also add that I hope you discover the uniqueness of Jesus this month.

Now, on with the show...1st of December, we're ready for you!

REDEEMING OUR HOME

Day 1: Advent as 'Coming Home'

Advent, for our family, is a season full of traditions.

I'd love to say that it's a time for increased spiritual growth, as I lead our young family in meaningful Bible reflections every morning – but in reality, I love present-wrapping, Christmas markets and Slade just as much as carol services, lighting our Advent candle and sharing the Christmas story together.

For all of December our house is full of mess and creativity: mince pies, boxes of decorations, *100 Carols for Choirs*, wreaths, Nativity figures, Lebkuchen (is there anything better?), glitter, paint, wrapping paper and ribbon. There is nothing about either the secular or religious versions of Advent that I don't embrace with arms open wide.

But Advent 2015 saw the arrival of a new tradition for us. Quite uncharacteristically, presents had been chosen, bought, wrapped and sent by mid-November. Why? Because on 1st December, our two youngest boys came home to us, having spent the first part of their short lives in foster care – so our Advent was taken up with learning how to care for toddlers again, whilst working out how to meet the needs of (no longer two, but) four children. There wasn't time for any more present wrapping.

It was a magical time in many ways. My husband spent most of December off work or working reduced hours. Kind friends provided evening meals for us right through the month. The excitement of Christmas kept cranking up for our older two, whilst our younger two gradually got used to their new environment, exploring and playing with increased confidence. And all four children enjoyed the novelty of having each other around for the first time, after months of waiting. I figured that January would bring more challenges (it did), but we enjoyed December while it lasted.

And so we added a new tradition. Advent means 'coming', and so now we always remember our boys 'coming home' at this time of year. This tradition reminds us that Advent is not just about the anticipation of Christmas, the first coming, but also about anticipation of the second coming – when Jesus will come again, and we, like our boys in 2015, will also *come home* to our forever home in God's kingdom, where we will be with God forever, never to be separated again.

> *For we know that if the earthly tent we live in is destroyed, we have a building from God, an eternal house in heaven, not built by human hands. Meanwhile we groan, longing to be clothed instead with our heavenly dwelling, because when we are clothed, we will not be found naked. For while we are in this tent, we groan and are burdened, because we do not wish to be unclothed but to be clothed instead with our heavenly dwelling, so that what is mortal may be swallowed up by life. Now the one who has fashioned us for this very purpose is God, who has given us the Spirit as a deposit, guaranteeing what is to come.*
> (2 Corinthians 5:1-5)

Advent, like adoption, opens our eyes to a new place, a *better place*, where the sin and suffering of the last place will be no more. Advent, like adoption, reminds us not to cling to our old home – not to get too settled here – because it's not where we belong. Advent, like adoption, tells us that the tragedies of this life are not supposed to bring us down, but to make us look up, waiting and hoping more desperately for a future in which destruction, lies, corruption, ill-health and death don't exist. Advent, like adoption, brings hope and a new start and a secure future. Advent, like adoption, prepares us for that glorious day when we will be with our true, heavenly Father.

Turning my eyes upwards, my December of roasted chestnuts, hot chocolate, hampers and tinsel has become the celebration which will one day be surpassed by an infinitely grander celebration, when all God's children *come home*.

> *In love he predestined us for adoption to sonship through Jesus Christ, in accordance with his pleasure and will— to the praise of his glorious grace, which he has freely given us in the One he loves.*
> (Ephesians 1:4-6)

- What is it about your current 'home' here on earth that you cling onto most tightly? (A relationship? Your physical home? A job? Your possessions?)

- How can you spend this Advent looking upwards with excitement for your eventual, eternal home?

Dear Lord, thank you that you have made me a wonderful home in heaven, where I will live for eternity with you, just as I was designed to. Please teach me the discipline of hope, that whilst I live on earth and suffer the results of sin and evil, I will trust you and your promise for the future. And if I am enjoying a blessed life right now, I pray that you would loosen my grip on the things around me and help me to enjoy them but not trust in them. Help me to cling to you more and more. Amen.

DAY 2: FROM RAGS TO RICHES

Yesterday I shared with you some of the Advent traditions that I love. But I left out one very important one: surely the most festive of festive Advent traditions – something that unites the nation in common love, adoration and hope.

Interviews night on The Apprentice.

I am a huge fan of this show. For the uninitiated, the show features a group of hopeful entrepreneurs who compete, week by week, for a £250,000 business investment from Lord Alan Sugar. At least one contestant gets fired each week, until there are just five left – at which point, instead of taking part in a business task, they are grilled by a handful of tough business types.

A few days before the interviews, an extra episode is aired, which takes a closer look at each of the five remaining candidates in the process, giving their back-story and business successes outside the TV show.

One thing which always intrigues me (and I've been watching this show for years) is how often the candidates have had a tough background, or suffered some personal tragedy. Some were raised by loving, but impoverished, single parents. Some tell a story of emigration to the UK from a traumatic situation in their country of origin. Abuse, health issues, bereavement, relationship breakdown – most, if not all, of these feature among the five candidates each year.

Of course the 'rags-to-riches' story makes for good television. But primarily this show isn't about the back-story – it only makes an appearance towards the end of the series – so I can't imagine that the producers choose the candidates on the basis of their backgrounds alone.

Instead, it seems that that having difficulties in life, particularly in childhood, can often make you stronger, more resilient and more determined. I've lost track of the number of Apprentice candidates over the years who've said, "I just want to provide a better life for my children," and who are clearly motivated by the very real memories of how tough life was for their own parents when they were growing up.

It's interesting that, although this is a fairly well-accepted line of thought regarding social or material success (i.e. that a tough background can often give you the drive to make something of yourself), it is a less-accepted line of thought when it comes to spiritual 'success'. If a difficult start in life has the potential to train you for future material success, is it not also true to say that experiencing some suffering might have the potential to shape us to be more like Christ? To achieve 'spiritual success'?

We regularly try to avoid any suffering for ourselves or for our kids, as that's how this world has programmed us – and the foundation for this approach is, after all, in the Bible. Our heavenly Father is a God of infinite love and patience, and commands us to parent our children likewise.

But what if there's another way of seeing suffering, and risk? These things, after all, are part of life and not always avoidable. What if some of that suffering is essential to developing Christ-like qualities in us, just as the Apprentice candidates' hard upbringings are essential to them developing the ambition that they need to succeed in business?

I know many stories of 'safe', middle-class Christian kids who have lost their faith in, or before, adulthood. And likewise, I could tell you many stories of Christian kids whose parents you might think had made rather questionable decisions on their behalf, yet grew into adults with a strong and distinctive faith of their own.

Nothing about Jesus' birth, childhood or adulthood was 'safe', in human terms. He didn't have all the advantages of financially secure parents. No further academic study. No home to call his own. Not even a 'respectable' temple-based career.

Even when Jesus was an adult, and able to make his own choices in life, he never chose the safe or expected way. The challenge is that he calls us to imitate him:

> *In your relationships with one another, have the same mindset as Christ Jesus:*
> *Who, being in very nature God,*

did not consider equality with God something to
be used to his own advantage;
rather, he made himself nothing
    by taking the very nature of a servant,
    being made in human likeness.
And being found in appearance as a man,
    he humbled himself
by becoming obedient to death – even death on a
cross!
Therefore God exalted him to the highest place
    and gave him the name that is above every
    name,
that at the name of Jesus every knee should bow,
    in heaven and on earth and under the earth,
and every tongue acknowledge that Jesus Christ is
Lord, to the glory of God the Father.
(Philippians 2:5-11)

Jesus is the ultimate rags-to-riches story. He made himself nothing (v.7) but is now 'exalted to the highest place' (v.9). Likewise, when we put our trust in Jesus, he turns our 'rags' – our suffering, our hardships, our difficulties in life – into a rich inheritance, a future in which we are raised to life, to live with God forever in a perfect eternity.

22

- In what ways do you seek worldly 'safety' and 'security' in your life?

- Is there something God is asking of you right now which may result in a harder journey than if you were to ignore his call? (If nothing comes to mind immediately, ask him – and spend some time waiting for his response!)

Lord Jesus, your life on earth was rich with meaning, saturated by wisdom, and ultimately fulfilling. I confess that I've spent so long enjoying the comforts and luxuries of this world that I've lost sight of what it means to be Christ-like. I've avoided your call when I suspect that it might involve suffering. I've tried to protect my kids blindly, rather than trusting them to your secure arms. Jesus, remove my blinkers. By your Holy Spirit, change me; fix my eyes unswervingly on you. In your precious name, Amen.

DAY 3: THE 'NOW AND NOT YET' OF ADVENT

If you have, or have ever had, small children in your life, you may be familiar with seeing a certain amount of impatience when it comes to Christmas.

One year, with more than a bit of frustration, my older son moaned, "I *wish* it was Christmas tomorrow!"

"Really?" I replied. "But then there'd be no Christmas fair, no Christmas jumper day, no Christingle, no decorating the house, no trip to see the lights, no Christmas stories, no Advent calendars, no school Christmas dinner, no class Christmas party...you wouldn't really want that, would you?"

He saw my point. Christmas Day can be a wonderful celebration of God sending Jesus to earth, but all the ways we celebrate in the preceding weeks are important too. They build up to the main event.

Waiting can be hard, can't it? The danger is that, like my son, we can be so desperate to get what we're waiting for that we miss out on what's happening here and now. I think he would have been pretty disappointed if we had just gone straight to Christmas Day and skipped all the fun stuff in December.

Likewise, if all we're ever focussed on is the day when Jesus will return and God will destroy sin and death forever, we're likely to miss out on a whole lot of fun stuff which he's doing right here, right now: the beauty of creation, the love of family and friends, growth in our personal holiness, the way a piece of art, music or theatre can speak deeply to us, the healing of physical conditions, or the joy of seeing a friend come to faith in Jesus.

Just before Jesus ascended to heaven, he warned his disciples of the danger of being too focussed on his return.

Then they gathered round...and asked him, 'Lord, are you at this time going to restore the kingdom to Israel?'

> *He said to them: 'It is not for you to know the times or dates the Father has set by his own authority. But you will receive power when the Holy Spirit comes*

on you; and you will be my witnesses in Jerusalem,
and in all Judea and Samaria, and to the ends of the
earth.'
(Acts 1:6-8)

God wants to redeem us all – our friends, our communities, our churches, our workplaces, and ourselves – through the transformative power of the Holy Spirit. Are we missing out on this because we're overly concerned with the end of time, when God will make all things right? As Jesus said, that's not our concern – it's God's. All we need to do is welcome the Holy Spirit into our lives to enable us to bear witness to Jesus Christ.

But there's a danger in the opposite approach too: sometimes we enjoy the wait so much that we lose sight of what we're actually waiting for.

A few years ago, we went with some friends to see the Tour de France come through our city. The waiting was fun – there was a bouncy castle for the kids, various freebies were being thrown out from passing advertising vehicles, and we had a plentiful supply of snacks to keep everyone happy. It was tempting to go home after an hour or so – after all, the kids were only young, they'd had a trip out and a bit of fun, so who was complaining? But that would have been to miss out on the whole point of why we were there.

When it came, it was quick (that's the point – it's a race) and it was over very soon. But the excitement that swelled through the crowd at that point was tangible, and we were thrilled to get caught up in it. I'm glad we didn't go home – we very nearly missed the main event because we'd had so much fun waiting!

Yesterday, we thought about how easy it is to sink back into the comforts of this world, rather than pursuing God's will – especially if we sense that God's will might involve some hardship. If we enjoy the wait so much, we forget who we were made for and where we were meant to live – and this is spiritually dangerous! In John 17, Jesus prays this for his disciples (but I think we can apply it to ourselves also, as modern-day disciples):

My prayer is not that you take them out of the world but that you protect them from the evil one. They are not of the world, even as I am not of it.

Sanctify them by the truth; your word is truth. As you sent me into the world, I have sent them into the world. For them I sanctify myself, that they too may be truly sanctified.
(John 17:15-19)

Jesus has *sanctified* us – made us holy, set us apart. We are not to cling so tightly to the things of this world that we stop being who God has called us to be. As we said on Day 1, we are not to get so comfortable here that we forget we were made for a heavenly home.

- Do you tend to focus more on Christ's return, or more on life in the here and now? Are you aware of how God is transforming you right now? If not, resolve to actively invite the Holy Spirit to work in you in the coming year!

- Think of one area where you need God's sanctifying power to make you more Christlike. (Often we don't notice that we've slotted into the world's way of doing things – so you may need to pray that God would help you to think of one way in which you have slotted in, and ask for his power to change.)

Dear Lord, this Advent, please keep my eyes open to the many wonderful things you're doing in my life, my church and my community. I praise you for your transformative power! Please continue to sanctify me – chip away at my character to make me more like the Christ whose birth I'm preparing to celebrate. Amen

DAY 4: THE THRILL OF THE RIDE

In this age of convenient online shopping experiences, untainted by human interaction, a trip to an Actual Shop can seem quite a highlight.

A few years ago, I found myself doing a bit of Christmas shopping in a well-known book shop. My Mum had requested a few books, so I found myself in the shop entrance, wondering *how the heck* you go about finding a specific title in a *REAL-LIFE BOOK SHOP.*

The newest titles were at the front, obviously, and I mentally kicked myself for not writing down the publication years of the books I was looking for. Assuming they weren't new releases, I headed further into store to the alphabetised shelves, and started to browse.

Book number one – no show. Book number two – not there. Book number three – missing. Just as I was wondering whether I had in fact misremembered my alphabet, a woman next to me struck up conversation.

"You know what's very good? Book Depository online. You just type in the title and it brings up the details."

"Yes...well I often use Wordery...but, you know, it's nice to support an actual shop, isn't it?" (And then, "Aha!" as I spotted the fourth book sitting unceremoniously on the shelf. Phew. Alphabet memory intact.)

"Well if you need anything, Book Depository is really excellent."

"Great, well, yes I do shop online *most* of the time, but just thought I'd use a real shop today, seeing as it's Christmas and all."

"Or do you know what else is good? Blackwell's online. Their website is excellent, very quick delivery."

It's tempting to take short cuts, isn't it? Not that there's anything wrong with saving a bit of time and money, and making the best of our resources. But if we apply such an efficiency model to our spiritual lives, we're in danger of missing out on something good.

I eventually found one of the books in the 'Crime' section. (The word 'murder' in the title should have given the game away.) And then, by complete chance, I found the remaining two on the 'Buy One Get One Half Price' table, after which I made my way to the till with my purchases, and enjoyed a brief but jovial bit of queue banter with an elderly gentleman about how *today of all days* was not the time to be closing the upstairs tills.

As I pondered the wasting of time and effort on things which could be done more quickly, I concluded that **the thrill is in the ride.** While it's tempting to long for heaven, and dream of what life will be like when God has defeated evil once and for all, we mustn't close our eyes to what God is doing in our lives and communities right now. While we wait for heaven, there is an adventure that God wants to take us on which beats any other way of living.

I could have typed four book titles into Google, and bought them all within seconds. Quick, efficient, easy – job done. But then I'd have missed out on the fun of going to a real bookshop – the sight and smell of *all those books*, the quirky conversations, the weight of the novels in my bag – as opposed to an 'order confirmation' email being pinged to my inbox. Not quite the same, is it?

It cost me more time and money to go to a real shop than to buy online. And it will cost us more to follow Christ daily than to live in a spiritual bubble of future dreams. But it was so much more enjoyable, unpredictable, and interesting to go to the bookshop. How much more, then, is life with Christ? It's impossible to say what exciting journeys, twists and turns God will take you on next – it'll be different for everyone – but I can promise that it will be thrilling.

> *Then Jesus said to his disciples, 'Whoever wants to be my disciple must deny themselves and take up their cross and follow me. For whoever wants to save their life will lose it, but whoever loses their life for me will find it. What good will it be for someone to gain the whole world, yet forfeit their soul? Or what can anyone give in exchange for their soul?'*
> (Matthew 16:24-26)

Yes, we know who's ultimately won the battle of everything – and yes, we know (roughly) what will happen at the end of this life. But the excitement is in how we get there. Don't opt for convenience – you might miss the thrill of the ride.

- Take a minute to think back over the last year: what unusual or unexpected things has God done or allowed in your life? It might be something in your family life, work environment, or an unexpected new friend coming into your life.

- Meditate on the passage from Matthew, above. In what way are you needing to 'deny yourself' right now?

Father God, thank you that you love me enough to guide me in the right way, even when it means pulling me away from things which seem attractive and secure. Thank you that what you offer is so much more thrilling. Please help me to see that this Advent, and to steer towards you at every turn. Amen.

DAY 5: THE AGONY OF THE RIDE

Yesterday, I shared the joy of going into a real, live bookshop.

My encounter ended well – very well. I got face-to-face encounters and felt the joyful weight of books in my hands. Compared to the alternative – a few taps on my phone, and a package through my door a few days later – my bookshop jaunt ended with a far greater sense of satisfaction and fulfilment.

But it didn't always feel satisfying, or victorious, or joyful. When I was floundering in the A-Z section, unable to find anything I was looking for, my mind (and the woman next to me) started to say: *You should have looked online. This would have been much quicker on Wordery. Why not leave it and buy later, from the comfort of your own home?*

We flounder in our Christian lives, too. We can't see where we're supposed to be heading, and the bit we're in currently can feel dark and hard, with an infinite number of questions and doubts. We really wish, sometimes, that we could take an alternative path. *You should just do what everyone else is doing.*

Things would be so much easier if you weren't trying to follow Christ. Why don't you just take that short-cut?

As we reflect on how this year has been for us, whilst looking towards the baby Christ in the manger, let's remember that Jesus never promised an easy life:

> *Enter through the narrow gate. For wide is the gate and broad is the road that leads to destruction, and many enter through it. But small is the gate and narrow the road that leads to life, and only a few find it.*
> (Matthew 7:13-14)

It certainly can be tempting to take the easier, broader, more comfortable road. But God offers us the road which will be most beneficial to us, and more glorifying to him, in the long term. He doesn't always give us what we want, and that's because he holds the long-term view that we lack. We want what is good in the here-and-now – but he wants what is best for us forever.

Amazingly, it is often during the times when everything feels like a long, hard slog, that we grow the most. It is often after these times that we look back and see clearly what God was teaching us. And, if these times seem to drift on and on, with no obvious feeling of getting through them, we often find that God is drawing us closer to him, honing and refining our character to be more like him. (Remember the 'rags-to-riches' idea from Day 2?)

As we read in Matthew 7, there is a road that leads to life – and, ultimately, that road is where I want to be, hard and dark though it may sometimes feel. God allows suffering into our lives and uses it to draw us closer to him, and to achieve his purposes for all mankind across history, which we can't begin to see from our limited perspective. Perhaps he is using your suffering to change the lives of others, or even to effect change for a generation.

While we may not be grateful now, we have a perfect future to look forward to in God's Kingdom – a future in which we won't regret a single pain or upset that we endured for the sake of pursuing God. Finally, we will see what crown our suffering has borne. How exciting to think that what we experience now could have an eternal impact in heaven!

- Whether you're travelling a difficult part of the road at the moment, or you can remember a time when you were, or you feel that your entire Christian life seems to be made up of sacrifices and suffering, spend a few moments in silence, asking God what he wants to teach you today.

Dear Father, thank you that your Son, born humbly in a manger, would grow up to be our Saviour. Thank you that, whatever suffering I'm enduring, he has suffered more. I can't express how astounded I am to know that you would make that sacrifice for me, but I want it to shape how I respond to life. Please help me to put you first over comfort, ease, security and convenience. Amen.

DAY 6: ARE YOU PREPARED?

Have you ever had Christmas-gift-wrap envy?

Don't laugh – it's A Real Thing. I expect there are support groups for it.

You think your presents look fine – until you see everyone else's. Their paper is smarter and more contemporary. There are ribbons and bows and gift bags and heartfelt messages on handmade tags - whereas my presents look like they've been wrapped by a helicopter propeller. (They haven't, but such is the effect when you try and wrap something whilst being simultaneously used as a landing pad for two energetic toddlers.)

One year, in the post-Christmas sales, I found myself snapping up half-price rolls of quality department-store paper, in order to try and up my game for the following year. It became something of a habit – an addiction, even – which I only discovered in late January, when I counted my spoils.

Do you know how much paper I had?

FORTY-THREE METRES.

We do have large families, but...*FORTY-THREE METRES???* I could wrap our entire house .

In short, I think you could say I was well-prepared for wrapping gifts the following Christmas.

Yes, I am pathetically materialistic. Guilty as charged. But I offer up this insane example of Christmas 'preparation' (or, maybe, *over*-preparation) to ask you – and me – the question: are we prepared?

I don't mean for Christmas. If you're one of those people who has everything bought and wrapped by mid-October, well done you. I will never be one of those people. And perhaps I hate you a little.

But really it doesn't matter in the slightest whether you're early or late with your preparations for December 25th. The big question is: are you ready to meet with Jesus this Christmas, and beyond? Are you ready to have your life transformed by him? And – if you have already met him – are you ready to listen to what he has to say to you next?

In *Joy to the World*, we sing:

"Let earth receive her King; Let every heart prepare him room."

Advent is about preparing and waiting. Preparing to celebrate Christ's birth – but also preparing for the time when he will come again to bring home those who have responded to his offer of a relationship with the living God.

Over the last few days we've been considering what it means to realign our self-centred and world-focussed selves to become God-centred and Kingdom-focussed. But how do we do that? What preparations do we need to make?

The apostle Peter said it so well in his speech to the crowd following the coming of the Holy Spirit at Pentecost, that I'm going to hand over to him. Be encouraged and challenged, as you read these words in the context of preparing your heart for Jesus this Christmas.

...Jesus of Nazareth was a man accredited by God to you by miracles, wonders and signs, which God did among you through him, as you yourselves know. This man was handed over to you by God's

deliberate plan and foreknowledge; and you, with the help of wicked men, put him to death by nailing him to the cross. But God raised him from the dead, freeing him from the agony of death, because it was impossible for death to keep its hold on him...

God has raised this Jesus to life, and we are all witnesses of it. Exalted to the right hand of God, he has received from the Father the promised Holy Spirit and has poured out what you now see and hear...

Therefore let all Israel be assured of this: God has made this Jesus, whom you crucified, both Lord and Messiah...

Repent and be baptized, every one of you, in the name of Jesus Christ for the forgiveness of your sins. And you will receive the gift of the Holy Spirit. The promise is for you and your children and for all who are far off – for all whom the Lord our God will call. (Acts 2:22-24, 32-33, 36, 38-39)

- Do we trust Jesus to be Lord of our lives? If so, are we ready to 'repent and be baptized'?

Or would we rather put our trust in our work, our family, and our friends?

- Are we preparing room in our lives for Jesus? Are we actively receiving God's gift of the Holy Spirit? Devote yourself to finding some time and space for Christ – now, and in the coming year

Jesus, I acknowledge with my lips that you are my King and my Saviour – but my life often does not reflect my testimony. From today, and into the next year, and beyond, please take your place on the central throne of my heart. And, from there, please transform my life by your Holy Spirit so that 'making room' for you is not only something I desire to do, but something I know I can't survive the rest of life without. Amen.

REDEEMING OUR CHRISTMAS

Day 7: What Are We Actually Celebrating?

Hint: no one's going to get any points if they say 'the birth of Christ.' Yes, of course I know that that *is* what Christmas is all about, and no, I haven't lost my marbles. At least, not all of them.

But the birth of Christ is so wide and broad in its impact. It was one day in history which had been prophesied for thousands of years previously, and which would change the course of history for thousands of years to come. It was the arrival of one tiny baby who grew up to be the only human being capable of bringing billions of human beings back into a relationship with the God who made them.

If Christmas is about the birth of Christ, then it is also about every way in which this affects our lives today. If we believe the coming of Jesus was a significant event, then what we are celebrating this year is not simply his birth, but the very many things that his birth represents.

So – what are you celebrating this Advent?

A few years ago, our eldest child started school, and we chose the school opposite our home which, at the time, was in special measures (that's the term for a failing school, if you're not familiar with the UK education system). I mean, you would, wouldn't you? We'd both been teachers, education was important to us – so why not risk a failing school? (Actually, there was a bit more to it than that – if you're interested, you can read the full story on my blog: 'Why I'm sending my kid to a school in special measures'.)

When our son started school, there was no PTA and hardly any fundraising events. Parents who had tried in previous years had become demoralised by a school which didn't welcome parental input.

But now, under new leadership, the school is in a different place. We have been able to establish a PTA and parents are much more involved. I've had the pleasure of organising the last couple of Christmas fairs, and they've raised a good amount for the school, as well as bringing together our wonderful community of children, families and staff for an afternoon of Christmassy fun.

(Oh, and in case you were interested, the school has improved – academically and pastorally – beyond what we would have thought possible a few years ago, and it recently received the rubber-stamp of a 'Good' Ofsted report rating.)

As long as I'm involved in organising PTA Christmas Fairs, what I will celebrate during Advent is the community that God is building at our school – the school which was so dire for so long, but now has a well-knitted team of children, staff, parents and governors, who are all rooting for each other.

True, love-filled community like this – with God and each other – is only possible because of Jesus:

> *A new command I give you: Love one another. As I have loved you, so you must love one another. By this everyone will know that you are my disciples, if you love one another.*
> (John 13:34-35)

What are you celebrating this Advent? A good idea might be to briefly review the last year. While I'm celebrating Jesus' gift of community, perhaps you, or a loved one, have experienced healing from a physical or mental condition. In that case, you might be celebrating that Jesus came to bring healing:

> *Then will the eyes of the blind be opened*

> *and the ears of the deaf unstopped.*
> *Then will the lame leap like a deer,*
> *and the mute tongue shout for joy.*
> (Isaiah 35:5–6a)

(Just a side note: perhaps you haven't experienced the healing you were praying for this year, and you're soldiering on with a painful condition, or grieving the loss of a loved one about whom, it would seem, your prayers were not answered. If this is you – hang on in there. I'm going to talk about suffering later this month. Today is about celebration – and I'm praying as I write this that you will be able to find something you can praise God for through your suffering.)

Jesus' birth also brought peace – perhaps something we can celebrate if we've enjoyed peaceful relationships with those around us this year:

> *Peace I leave with you; my peace I give you. I do not give to you as the world gives. Do not let your hearts be troubled and do not be afraid.*
> (John 14:27)

Perhaps your year has been full of joy or hope, or a situation you're involved in has seen justice; perhaps you've experienced a new depth of compassion for those around you, or a stronger reliance on God as your Father. Whatever your year has been like, praise God for sending Jesus to make these things possible!

- What are you celebrating this year? A new friendship, good health, the growth of a voluntary project or business venture?

- What has Jesus' birth brought you, relating to this? Community? Healing? Peace?

Dear Jesus, I praise you for your birth, and I praise you for all that it continues to mean in my life. This Christmas help me to reflect on your goodness to me this year, and remember to thank you for it. And though things in my life are not perfect, and there is still suffering, thank you that when you return again, you will bring us to a perfect home with you. Please keep my eyes fixed on this. Amen.

DAY 8: CAN ANYONE TELL WHAT YOU'RE CELEBRATING?

In our home, as perhaps in yours, there's always an argument about when the Christmas tree should go up. If he had his way, my husband would put it up on Christmas Eve and not a day earlier – whilst my son would have the house decorated for two months if we let him.

One November, we came down for breakfast to find that our boy had already made space in our lounge for the tree, in an effort to convince us that we really should start decorating. Given that fitting a tree into our lounge involves an armchair and a two-seater sofa trading places, and that our son was just eight at the time, it was a pretty determined action!

I do love decorations, whenever they go up. Many of them tell a story, reminding us of the person who gave it to us, the place we bought it, or the age of our children when they made it.

And I love the important story they tell: a story of love, of Christ, of 'God with us', of gentleness and compassion, of a God who stooped down to bring us back into his arms.

Except some decorations don't tell this story, do they? They tell of flying snowmen or mysterious men who arrive through your chimney, or helpful elves, or glittering reindeer.

There's nothing wrong with having secular decorations in your home or enjoying the secular celebrations of Christmas – in fact, I think many of them can increase our sense of joy and excitement at celebrating the birth of Christ. But if our Advent is more consumed with these celebrations than with Jesus, then I wonder what those around us will make of our faith. That it isn't joyful enough in itself? That we have to supplement it with more 'amazing' stories? That Christ's birth alone isn't *quite* enough to bring fulfilment?

For those of us with children, we need to ask ourselves what story of Christmas we want them to grow up with: something richly significant, full of depth and infinite lessons – or something plastic and fake, fun for a while, but which doesn't have an impact on the rest of the year?

Over recent years, I've gently steered towards having physical objects in our home which remind us of what we're celebrating during this season. Yes, we do Advent calendars, letters to Santa (more tomorrow) and Christmas dinners – but, through the haze of all this, I don't want my kids to grow up wondering if Santa was born in a manger, or whether Jesus had twelve reindeer.

In fact, I don't want anyone who enters our home this season to be in any doubt about what we're celebrating.

I've had to be creative. Sometimes I've bought decorations which point to the Nativity, and other times I've had to make them, because what I'm looking for doesn't exist in the shops. But I love it when I find something which can help our home point towards Jesus at Christmas – it's become a fun challenge every Advent!

In yesterday's chapter, we thought about what we would be celebrating this Christmas, and today we're thinking about the importance of making this obvious to those who observe our lives. There are some wonderful words in Deuteronomy which encourage us in this:

Love the Lord your God with all your heart and with all your soul and with all your strength.

These commandments that I give you today are to be on your hearts. Impress them on your children. Talk about them when you sit at home and when you walk along the road, when you lie down and when you get up. Tie them as symbols on your hands and bind them on your foreheads. Write them on the door-frames of your houses and on your gates.

(Deuteronomy 6:5-9)

It seems that this passage is saying our faith should be visible physically ("write them on the door-frames…"), in conversation ("talk about them…"), and in our actions ("Love the Lord your God…") – in other words, YES in our home, but not just limited to our homes! What is it about us, our characters, our actions, and our priorities, which makes our faith obvious to those around us? Are we seeking to be more Christ-like? Are we developing the fruits of the Spirit listed in Galatians 5?

53

- What are you **actually** celebrating this Christmas? And can anyone tell?

- Which **one** fruit of the Spirit are you most in need of right now? Ask God for it! (They are: love, joy, peace, patience, kindness, goodness, faithfulness, gentleness and self-control – try to limit yourself to just one!)

Lord God, thank you again for your great gift of Jesus, sent to be our Rescuer. Please equip me to pass this good news on to those around me. May my life reflect your truth, may my work and my actions reflect your goodness, and may my home be a place which points to you. Amen

DAY 9: HOW SANTA CAN DRAW US TO CHRIST

Yesterday, I mentioned that in our family we write letters to Santa. Some sections of the church might disown me for this! But I think we can learn a lot through Santa.

There is so much which is fun about Santa. He's a novelty – someone who turns up just once a year, but is friendly and kind, and delivers exactly the presents you've asked for, all wrapped up in a stocking or sack. How fun is that? And he doesn't just do this for you, but – somehow, miraculously – for *all* the children around the world.

The real 'Santa', St. Nicholas, was also a kind, friendly, generous man – he loved God, and from that relationship came a heart for the poor and vulnerable around him. The legend of him dropping three bags of gold into the slippers of three young women in his village whose father was too poor to afford their dowries – even if it may have been embellished down the years – shows a heart which was *sacrificially* generous. St. Nicholas didn't have much, but what he did have, he gave with joyful abandonment.

During Advent, we love to share this story with our kids and with each other. Santa was a real person, St. Nicholas, who was equipped by God to be generous. In telling this story, our kids have always known that Santa – as we celebrate him today – is not alive today, but that he *was* based on a real person. (We've also told them not to tell their classmates who may be enjoying a rather different story!)

This has not killed the magic for our family. On the contrary, it has added a rich significance to this fun tradition for kids – and it has protected them from any sense of feeling let-down by a man who promises more than he can deliver.

You see, Santa also has his failings. He only rewards you if you're good. He watches what you do through the year, and keeps a list of your wrongdoings. He's not interested in a relationship with you.

In short – Santa is only human. He cannot fulfil our deepest needs any more than our spouse, parents or children can. To base our Christmas around him would result in huge disappointment.

But if we celebrate Santa as St. Nicholas, the whole tradition can be redeemed to point to Jesus. St

Nicholas gave freely and sacrificially because he'd received freely and sacrificially from Jesus' death and resurrection – and that could not have happened without Jesus being born: the very event we're celebrating!

Baby Jesus grew up to be our Rescuer – the One who would put us right with God *forever.* He would not keep a record of our wrongdoings, but forgive us *freely* – and his gift would be available to *all,* regardless of how 'good' we were. As we remember St. Nicholas, the gracious man who gave of his money, time and energy, we are more able to look up to the God who inspired him.

Celebrating 'Santa' in this way is fun, rich and meaningful. But if we elevate Santa to a position above Jesus, this can result in muddied waters for our children, who don't realise who, what or why we're celebrating.

Alternately, if Jesus and Santa are celebrated equally, but separately, we run the risk of confusing our children (and ourselves) with two parallel, unrelated Christmas celebrations. Who is our real hero?

In Zechariah's day, God's people felt disappointed by their return to Israel. It wasn't all they had expected, so they started to grumble, and turned to idols. But, through Zechariah, God made it very clear that these idols had **no power** whatsoever, and that His people needed to return to Him, who was able to do all things:

Ask the Lord for rain in the springtime;
it is the Lord who sends the thunderstorms.
He gives showers of rain to all people,
   and plants of the field to everyone.
The idols speak deceitfully,
   diviners see visions that lie;
they tell dreams that are false,
   they give comfort in vain.
Therefore the people wander like sheep
   oppressed for lack of a shepherd.
(Zechariah 10:1-2)

In today's terms, an 'idol' is anything which diverts our attention from God. Often it's the most innocuous, innocent parts of our culture which have the most potential to draw us away from Jesus. Is Santa – or any of the more 'secular' traditions – threatening to shift your focus this Christmas? Or are you able to use them to glorify Jesus even more?

- If you have children, think back over the last few days, and those coming up. How many of your activities/celebrations have been about Santa? How many about Jesus? Or do you combine the two?

- As an adult, what are the secular Christmas traditions (like Santa) which threaten to draw your attention from Jesus?

Lord God, you've commanded me not to make idols - and yet I do it unthinkingly in so many ways, not least at Christmas when all the festivities claim my attention and focus. Please re-orientate my gaze onto you, trusting in you for the satisfaction I can't find elsewhere. Amen.

DAY 10: TRADITIONS AND SURPRISES

You already know how much I love Christmas traditions, and yesterday I shared how we can use the tradition of Santa to celebrate Jesus even more at Christmas. I wonder what kind of traditions you and your family enjoy. Do you always have a gathering of extended family or friends on a particular day? Do you have a bizarre trimming to the Christmas dinner, or an alternative pudding, that only your family serves up?

Some traditions are so old that no one can remember how they started. In my family, we have the 'Baynes Family Chorus', a totally bizarre and ultimately meaningless rhythmic chant performed with claps, arm slaps, elbows and hand-banging the table (after the big meal, of course – the aim is to get the cutlery and glassware clattering to the extent that the host feels on the edge of a nervous breakdown). No one knows where it originated, or who started it, but we've done it every Christmas that I can remember, and now my kids are learning it.

Many of the traditions you and I follow contain some element of surprise – for example, wrapping presents, hanging up stockings, surprise days out. A couple of years ago, my brother-in-law, a Liverpool FC season ticket holder, arranged to take our footie-mad son to Anfield on Boxing Day – it was the largest stadium and most significant match he'd been to, and we kept it a surprise till Christmas Day. He had an unforgettable time!

I love the idea of tradition and surprise sitting side-by-side. One is predictable; the other is not. I think we need both in our Christmas celebrations.

We need traditions, because the Christmas story happened a long time ago. We need predictable, enjoyable and successful ways to tell and re-tell the story, passing it on from generation to generation – whether through carols, the giving of cards and presents, sharing particular foods, or even having a few glasses smashed by a rowdy family stabbing their elbows onto the dinner table in unison.

We also need surprise – because the Christmas story was full of surprises, and yet over the years we've lost our sense of amazement at how Jesus was born. Perhaps if we take a look at some of the surprise elements of the story, we'll be able to rekindle that 'wow' factor of seeing something we've never seen before.

Firstly, there's the means by which God chose to send his son – born not in a palace to a royal family, or even in a nice detached home to a well-to-do family – but to vulnerable parents in a stable.

Mary, Joseph and the shepherds were all surprised to be visited by angels. (Well, you would be, wouldn't you?)

And there were shepherds living out in the fields nearby, keeping watch over their flocks at night. An angel of the Lord appeared to them, and the glory of the Lord shone around them, and they were terrified. But the angel said to them, "Do not be afraid. I bring you good news that will cause great joy for all the people. Today in the town of David a Saviour has been born to you; he is the Messiah, the Lord. This will be a sign to you: you will find a baby wrapped in cloths and lying in a manger."
(Luke 2:8-12)

The shepherds were equally surprised to find the baby lying in a manger, exactly as the angels had said

– and the wise men were pretty surprised not to find Jesus at Herod's palace.

When the wise men eventually found Jesus by following the star, I bet Mary and Joseph were pretty surprised by the impressive presents these important figures had brought for their tiny son.

Jesus didn't stop surprising people throughout his life. When the Pharisees believed they had it right – staying away from disease and impurity – Jesus surprised them by touching the sick and dining with prostitutes. When the disciples tried to tactfully move a bunch of children away from Jesus, he surprised everyone by welcoming them, blessing them, and even telling the adults that *they* were the ones who needed to learn from these children. When a promiscuous woman was gathering her water for the day, Jesus surprised her not only by striking up a conversation (a cultural no-no) but by telling her everything she'd ever done – and forgiving her.

- Have you been surprised by Jesus? If not, take some time this month to read one of the most culturally shocking stories about Jesus: try Matthew 19:16-30, Luke 5:27-32 or John 4.

And this is just a small sample. Read a whole gospel and you'll count dozens of ways Jesus surprised his contemporaries.

- Which traditions do you have (or can you start) which help to re-capture some of the 'surprise' elements of Jesus' birth? (I'll start you off: wrapping presents, opening an Advent calendar, using a story bag to tell the Christmas story to children.)

Lord Jesus, from your birth to your death and glorious resurrection, you were constantly surprising those around you. Today, I confess that I don't always allow myself to feel just how counter-cultural you were, and still are. Please surprise me, this Advent, with an aspect of your character or teaching - and may it change my life in distinctive ways. Amen.

DAY 11: JOY TO THE WORLD

While wrapping presents, I like to whack on some Christmas music. One of my favourite Christmas albums is by the Post-Modern Jukebox – and hands-down my favourite song on that album is 'Joy to the World'. It's a great, uplifting carol anyway, but the Motown arrangement, exuberant vocals and enthusiastic tambourine really give it a toe-tapping sense of amazement and wonder that's highly contagious.

You see, the words of this carol already express some of the amazement the shepherds would have felt, on hearing that their Saviour had come – but this sense of wonder doesn't come naturally to me today, two millennia after the event. Re-thinking the song's arrangement has also helped me to re-think my attitude to the (still amazing) news that my Saviour has come.

Yesterday, we talked about the element of surprise in the Christmas story. To say the shepherds would have been surprised to see angels is an understatement. But look at the powerful words with which the angels announce Jesus' birth:

...I bring you good news that will cause great joy for all the people. Today in the town of David a Saviour has been born to you; he is the Messiah, the Lord...
(Luke 2:10-11)

To the shepherds – poor, uneducated, untrusted, side-lined members of society – this news meant everything. Would this Saviour be the One who would rescue them from the Roman government, from their station in life, from the disease and death which were a regular part of their lives? If so, then 'good news' and 'great joy' were indeed what was being promised!

The shepherds certainly experienced great joy (they 'hurried off' to Bethlehem, didn't they?), but I wonder why we don't feel the same when we contemplate the Christmas story? After all, the good news hasn't changed. Why do we not get so excited to have a 'Saviour', a 'Messiah', who will literally be 'God to the rescue' for us?

As I said yesterday, I guess good news dulls over time. We've known this truth all our lives; even if we haven't believed it to be true (or still don't), we've always known about the historical figure of Jesus. It is no longer 'news' like it was to the shepherds, that very first Christmas.

But I think there's another reason why we don't feel the joy of the shepherds. They knew how much they were in need of a Messiah. They knew they couldn't enter God's presence apart from time-consuming and costly rituals. They knew that their wrongdoings would always come between them and a God who was 100% holy. They *needed* rescuing – and they knew it. It had been foretold for hundreds of years, but perhaps they'd given up hope that this Rescuer would ever come.

Our own recognition of how much we need a Saviour has also faded through the years. We've devised systems and structures to distract us from the existence of God and our need for an unbroken relationship with him. We have built walls to give ourselves security and protection, trusting in our economy, our careers, our salaries, our house-purchases – or, if it all falls through, the welfare state. We have layers upon layers of people around us who we hope will meet our emotional needs, provide financial stability, help us move up the career ladder, and so on.

But strip it all away, and at the core of our being is a deep yearning to be in close contact with the One who made us. And the external things in which we put our trust? They might provide income, a temporary security, the keeping up of appearances – but they don't deal with the heart of the problem: **we can never be perfect, and we need rescuing from ourselves.**

Jesus – humble, peace-loving, revolutionary – came to lead us to God. He came to show us that we need a Rescuer. He took the horrific punishment that should have been ours – the punishment deserved by all humankind from the start of time to the end because of our wrongdoing – and he ended the grip that our failures have over us. Only he could take this punishment, as only he was perfect – if he wasn't, then his death would only have paid his own debt, not ours.

Let's not forget, this Advent, that we need rescuing. Perhaps then we will start to sense some of the amazement of the shepherds, and be able to sing "joy to the world" with true excitement!

- Spend a few minutes remembering how much you need rescuing, then meditating on the amazing news that your Rescuer has COME! There is hope!

Dear Lord, Is it really true? Have you really sent a Saviour to rescue me? What love, what sacrifice! Thank you for giving me a way out of the mess of this life. Please grow in me a sense of exuberant joy this Advent, and give me opportunities to speak and sing about how wonderful this is! Amen.

DAY 12: THE FEAST

At this point in December, I often feel like I'm spending more time in the supermarket than in my own home. Short of taking a sleeping bag and toothbrush with me, I've basically taken up residency in Morrisons.

After all, there's a lot of food to source in December. Even when we're not hosting the Big Day, there are still class Christmas parties which need food contributions, a heck of a lot of homemade sweets and treats to make, family and friends popping round expecting nibbles – and of course normal, everyday meals, which still have to happen somehow. No sooner has one event passed, than another presents itself, requiring yet another trip to the shops.

When I have the choice of products, or quantities, I tend to over-cater. *(Which flavour? We'll get both. Three ice-cream tubs or four? Best go for five.)* I really don't want to run out of anything and be doing these supermarket-runs when people are staying, even though we all know I've ordered too much.

Exuberance, as long as it doesn't put us into debt or create unhealthy amounts of food waste, does feel like an appropriate way to celebrate a Christian festival. We wouldn't eat like this all year, but it's absolutely right to celebrate the coming of God's King with a nod towards the plenty of that Kingdom.

All the abundance, decadence and extravagance that we can muster at Christmas time *does not come close* to the great riches we will one day inherit from our heavenly Father. It's only a very, *very* faint substitute. But it serves as a tangible, physical, memorable reminder that one day, thanks to Jesus' birth and sacrifice, we will feast with him in heaven.

We love all the verses that speak of this abundance, don't we?

They feast in the abundance of your house; you give them drink from your river of delights.
(Psalm 36:8)

You crown the year with your bounty, and your carts overflow with abundance.
(Psalm 65:11)

...I have come that they may have life, and have it to the full.

(John 10:10)

But there's another aspect to the heavenly feast which we often overlook. In Luke, Jesus gives this warning:

When you give a luncheon or dinner, do not invite your friends, your brothers or sisters, your relatives, or your rich neighbours; if you do, they may invite you back and so you will be repaid. But when you give a banquet, invite the poor, the crippled, the lame, the blind, and you will be blessed. Although they cannot repay you, you will be repaid at the resurrection of the righteous.

(Luke 14:12-14)

In this passage, Jesus goes on to tell the story of a man who prepared a great banquet, but none of his friends would come.

He told his servant to go into the streets to invite *"the poor, the crippled, the blind and the lame"* (v.21) – and, when there was still space, he widened the invitation:

*Go out to the roads and country lanes and compel
them to come in, so that my house will be full.*
(Luke 14:23)

God's heavenly banquet is wildly inclusive. We
Christians like to talk about inclusivity, but I'm not
sure we quite understand it the way God does. Are
we willing to invite into our homes those who are
struggling with alcohol and drug addictions, or living
on the streets, or have a known criminal record?

Our extravagant celebrations at Christmas can be a
great opportunity to practise hospitality, and involve
those on the fringes. This might not necessarily mean
someone who it's hard to have in your home – it
could be a good friend who you wouldn't dream of
not asking but who, without your invitation, would be
on their own.

Who in your community needs to experience some
lavish, unconditional love, poured out in good food
and good company? Who in your community has
never enjoyed Christmas? Inviting someone to play
charades with your family for an afternoon might not
seem very special – but it might just impact your
guest for eternity.

With hospitality comes acceptance. *You are accepted in our home. Your presence is wanted. You are valued and loved.* It is a glimpse towards the Kingdom we will one day inherit.

- The heavenly feast will be abundant! Are you in danger of scrimping unnecessarily this Christmas as you celebrate? (Note: I'm not talking to those of you who are on a tight budget – I would never advocate going into debt for this. But to those of you who can afford to be generous: do your celebrations reflect the exuberant Saviour you serve?)

- The heavenly feast will be inclusive! Are you in danger of only trusting close friends and family to enter your home? Ask God to bring to mind people He would like you to welcome in.

Jesus Christ, you came into the world to point to the Kingdom of God, and to give us a way to get there. I praise you for your sacrifice. In my celebrations over the next few days, please help me to orientate the extravagance towards you, using it both as an opportunity to thank you for your provision throughout the year, and a chance to bless others by showing them a little of how much they mean to you. Thank you that, one day, we will experience a feast which is wilder than anything we could dream up here on earth. Amen.

REDEEMING OUR HEARTS

DAY 13: A PERFECTLY IMPERFECT ADVENT

Do you ever have days sponsored by Calpol (or the medicinal drug of your choice)?

They're rubbish, aren't they? You have to miss things you were looking forward to and people you were looking forward to seeing. You end up watching loads of telly, which starts off as a nice way to relax, but eventually gives you sore eyes and a restless feeling of having missed out on Real Life for a day. The house is a mess, but you can do precious little about it, as you're feeling too rough (or are caring for someone who's feeling rough) to get off the sofa, let alone wield a broom.

I have a piece of stunning insight to share with you, from all my years on this planet. **Advent is not immune to imperfection.**

You're welcome.

We still get ill in December, we still have marital arguments in December, homes still get robbed in December, loved ones still die in December.

The Christmas adverts show such perfect children, homes, Christmas trees, dinner tables and toys that I always hope that if we keep the telly on for long enough, the spirit of perfection will seep out into our messy home. Sadly, it's never happened.

But, actually, I often find that imperfect days are splattered with wonderful moments too. I recall one day during Advent when my youngest boys and I were feeling under the weather. Despite missing our usual groups, we had a lovely time of Christmassy craft at home, and enjoyed two separate visits from two separate friends – the type of friends who enrich my life and fill my emotional tank whenever I spend time with them. They listen, they ask the right questions, their conversation is interesting and wise and seasoned with grace. *And* I can totally be myself around them – no worrying about how messy the house is, or if I'm still padding around in PJs, or if I'm serving up Aldi freezer food for tea.

I'm willing to bet most of you will have already experienced some imperfections this Advent, and I want you to be encouraged. It's these kinds of perfectly imperfect days, far from the Pinterest world of minimalist homes, stylishly dressed kids, crafts you could sell on Etsy, and home-cooked suppers, which cause me to relate to the Christmas story so much more.

And that's because the first Christmas was perfectly imperfect too. No one chooses to give birth in a stable. And – sorry, men – most women prefer to give birth in the presence of someone who has a small clue what they're doing. Also no one really wants strangers turning up unannounced in the early days, when every feed hurts like crazy and basically involves a very un-sexy strip show in order to get the right latch.

But it was also perfect. It was, in every way, what God had planned. A humble birth, a humble boy, a humble family. Special visitors – from the poorest (shepherds) to the richest (wise men) – because the Son of God had come for *everyone,* regardless of background. And this had been prophesied hundreds of years before:

> But you, Bethlehem Ephrathah,
> though you are small among the clans of Judah,
> out of you will come for me
> one who will be ruler over Israel,
> whose origins are from of old,

from ancient times.
(Micah 5:2)

Bethlehem was a *non-place.* The dregs of the earth. What good could come from there? But God had it all planned. *The perfectly-imperfect plan.* It was meant to be.

As we wait for Christmas this Advent, remembering the perfectly-imperfect birth of Jesus, our Rescuer, we also wait for the time when he will come back to earth – and, once and for all, rid the world of imperfections.

That really will be perfect.

- In what area/s of your life do you strive for perfection? The desire to do things well is not necessarily wrong, as long as we're keeping God in the centre – but if the striving is wearing you down, bring this to God now in prayer.

Lord Jesus, your birth – planned by God – was perfect. Perfectly timed, perfectly recorded. This Christmas, please help me to cling to your perfection, and lay more and more of my imperfections at your feet. Amen.

DAY 14: THE ADVENT DISASTER

Advent is not immune to imperfection – and it is not immune to disaster.

Let me be clear, my definition of an Advent disaster falls into the same category as the accepted definition of a First World Problem: something totally banal and inconsequential which has more significance as an anecdote than it ever had as an event. Humour me: I'm a writer. This is how I roll.

I'll give you some examples of Advent disasters. A tree decoration gets broken. Homemade fudge doesn't set. Nativity figures go missing (ever tried telling the story without Mary?) You get ill on the day you were supposed to be taking the kids to the panto.

But sometimes, of course, the disasters are much more serious. A family argument which results in Christmas Day plans being changed. The news that a work contract won't be extended into the new year. The realisation that finances are running dangerously low. Some bad news from the doctor.

As we saw yesterday, December's celebratory edge does not, unfortunately, make it immune to suffering.

The good news is that we have a God who is not afraid of facing disasters head-on. I can say this with confidence, because there were disasters aplenty around the time of Jesus' birth. The great event was not only imperfect (see yesterday's chapter), but smattered with full-on disasters too. God could have sent his Son in a much simpler and easier way – but he didn't.

In an age where giving birth out of wedlock would make you a social outcast, Jesus' parents weren't married when Mary's pregnancy was announced.

Then there was the long journey, decreed by an insecure, power-crazy government, which had to be taken at just the moment where Mary was due to give birth.

And did I mention the fleeing from a tyrannical King, and the fact that Jesus and his family became refugees? Yep, that too.

Bringing God's Son into the world was no straightforward event. But none of these disasters had the power to change history. None of them could prevent the Son of God himself being born as a tiny baby, who would grow up to model life as God intended it, then suffer a cruel death in our place, and rise from it in a glorious victory which would defeat death forever for those who believe in him.

For I am convinced that neither death nor life, neither angels nor demons, neither the present nor the future, nor any powers, neither height nor depth, nor anything else in all creation, will be able to separate us from the love of God that is in Christ Jesus our Lord.
(Romans 8:38-39)

Did you read that? Nothing can separate us from God's love! Nothing we go through in the future, nothing we've done in the past, no people, no death (our own, or of those close to us) – absolutely nothing can separate us from God's love. He *wants* to love us, and no one is going to stop him!

And this includes disasters. No disaster, big or small, could prevent God from sending his Son down to earth to love us, and no disaster has yet succeeded in separating us from the love of God's Son, as long as we're choosing to accept it.

This doesn't mean, though, that the obstacles surrounding Jesus' birth were unforeseen, catching God unaware as if he hadn't accounted for any problems. On the contrary, they were entirely part of the plan, and they actually *help* us to grab hold of the Christmas story and relate to it.

Jesus knows the ups and downs of life because he lived them – right from day one. He knows what it's like to be rejected, cast out of society, a refugee, and homeless.

Think about it. If Jesus' parents were already married, how would they have learnt to trust God above the traditions and customs of their culture? According to etiquette, Joseph was meant to divorce Mary quietly. But God had other plans, and Joseph needed to learn to put God above his reputation.

If Jesus had been born in a palace, how would he have been able to relate to normal, working people? And how would he have been able to start his teaching ministry at the age of 30, if he had been born into a family with its own expectations of how his entire adult life would pan out?

If Jesus had never been a refugee, how would he have been able to speak about the poor or marginalised with such integrity? How would he have been content to be homeless for three years, teaching the disciples to go where they were welcomed, receive what was given to them with thanks, and move on from places where they were rejected?

This is the Jesus who invites us to get to know him this Christmas. It was all part of God's plan – the disasters, everything. And there is nothing in your life right now which God can't use to draw you closer to him and to achieve his will on earth.

- Meditate on the passage from Romans above. Is there anything in your life right now which feels like it might separate you from the love of God in Jesus? Share it with God now in prayer, and be reassured that it has no such power!

Dear Lord, thank you for assuring me of your love. Thank you that nothing can separate me from it. You know my situation, and the temptations pulling me away from you. Please be glorified through whatever I am going through today, and help me to draw nearer to you as a result. Amen.

DAY 15: A COSMOS-SIZED RESPONSIBILITY

Parenting is a huge responsibility.

When you discover the blue lines on the pregnancy test, it can be pretty overwhelming to realise that you have a whole new life *growing inside you*. Mums start to take better care of themselves; Dads become more protective – because there's a growing sense of the responsibility with which they've been entrusted.

Once the baby is actually born, there's a whole new set of tasks and routines to learn, and it can all feel quite daunting. Is he getting enough milk? Am I winding him right? Did I leave his nappy on too long?

And when you've mastered these tasks, when they start to fade into a distant memory as your child grows up, there presents a greater awareness of needing to raise a good, kind human-being who makes a positive contribution to society. This responsibility too can feel heavy and burdensome.

Have you ever considered what a *huge* responsibility it would have been for Mary and Joseph to raise the

Son of God? Not much is written in the Bible about Jesus' childhood, but think of all the decisions his parents would have made for him on a daily basis. *How can I get him to eat vegetables? When should we potty-train him? Which bad habits need to be broken? Which battles should I fight?*

Making these decisions can be difficult at the best of times – but knowing you're making them for the Messiah?

Yep, exactly.

I don't know how fazed Mary and Joseph actually were – did parenting the Son of God come naturally to them? Or did they, from time to time, flip out?

I'm pretty sure I know what I would have done.

The Bible tells us very little about Jesus' childhood, but there's one story which provides valuable encouragement to us when we feel ill-equipped to deal with our own responsibilities, be they child-rearing, management, caring for elderly relatives, church ministry, or anything else God has allowed in our lives. Let's take a look at it:

When [Jesus] was twelve years old, they went up to the [Passover] festival, according to the custom. After the festival was over, while his parents were returning home, the boy Jesus stayed behind in Jerusalem, but they were unaware of it. Thinking he was in their company, they travelled on for a day. Then they began looking for him among their relatives and friends. When they did not find him, they went back to Jerusalem to look for him. After three days they found him in the temple courts, sitting among the teachers, listening to them and asking them questions. Everyone who heard him was amazed at his understanding and his answers. When his parents saw him, they were astonished. His mother said to him, "Son, why have you treated us like this? Your father and I have been anxiously searching for you."

"Why were you searching for me?" he asked. "Didn't you know I had to be in my Father's house?" But they did not understand what he was saying to them.

Then he went down to Nazareth with them and was obedient to them. But his mother treasured all these things in her heart. And Jesus grew in wisdom and stature, and in favour with God and man.
(Luke 2:42-52)

Mary and Joseph were pretty stressed out – and understandably so. Their boy, not yet a teenager, had left their walking party, and caused a huge amount of panic about where he might be, or what might have happened to him. Would he ever understand how worried his parents were?

Whatever might be stressing you out at the moment, it's okay to feel panicked. God knows, and he's got your back. Whatever you are holding in life right now, however precariously balanced it feels, God is holding you – and so, he's holding everything you hold. Just as God helped Mary and Joseph to be the parents Jesus needed them to be, so he is helping you to cope with your responsibilities, providing time and energy to get everything done, and offering grace for those moments when things fall through the cracks.

This is the time of year when many of us feel additional stress. Mediating between relatives who don't get on, having the same old disagreements with a spouse about what budget is reasonable for Christmas presents, dealing with tantrums and meltdowns from over-excited, over-tired children. And all in addition to the stresses and strains we're already bearing.

God knows this. And he's there with us, guiding us through. Yes, we need to submit it all to him. But that sometimes feels like a pat answer which doesn't actually offer any practical solution.

If we are to really know the presence of Immanuel – God with us – this Christmas, we need to talk to him for sure. But we also need to listen. We are told that Mary *"treasured all these things in her heart"* – but how often do we allow ourselves the space and time necessary to ponder all that God is doing and teaching us?

As we submit our responsibilities, our burdens and commitments to God, and as we wait for his guidance, we will find wonderful things starting to happen. They might not be dramatic or immediate. It may be a gradual in-dwelling of peace, as you start to realign your priorities, or it may be a clear sense of needing to lay down a commitment, or a realisation that the thing you were concerned about is not actually as important as it seemed at first. But he will work, and you will grow, and this time next year you may have a beautiful story to share!

- What are your responsibilities right now? Which ones are making you stressed or worried? It may help you to write a list.

Lord God, you gave Mary and Joseph a huge responsibility, but you equipped them to deal with it. Likewise, you know the responsibilities you have given me, or allowed me to experience. Please help me to carry them with grace and love. Please give me the time and the energy to fulfil the commitments I have. I lay them down with you now. If there is anything I need to lay aside, or any priorities I need to realign, please bring them to mind now. Amen.

DAY 16: STICK TO THE GRID

Like every other Christmas activity, present-wrapping makes my heart sing a happy song. The thrill of hiding something from curious eyes, feeling their owner's excitement build until it seems they might burst for not knowing, keeps me going when the pile of things to wrap seems unlikely to diminish.

Yet one thing gets me just a little bit grumpy.

The Grid.

You know what I mean – those stupid criss-cross lines on the reverse side of the gift-wrap. These little bad boys are the bane of my life during Advent.

They stare up at me with the unfaltering expression of a hard-nosed schoolmistress, ready to judge my every cut and tear.

I'll tell you why I don't get on with them. *They're never going to work.* Straight lines, marked out on a material which has been rolled up for months, are about as useful as a pen-knife in a shark attack.

The lines are straight, but the paper is not. You try and stick to the grid, but you end up with something resembling a dinosaur's back – if the paper hasn't already ripped before you've reached the other side. It seems to me that *any* roll of wrapping paper knows exactly where and how it intends to be cut, and damned if you're going to foil its plans.

All sorts of proverbial 'grids' are marked out for us in life too – and they seem equally impossible to follow. Whether it's the grid for how you should do education, who you should love, when you should marry, how many kids you should have, or how your career should pan out, the world around us loves to give us a grid to follow.

Even in the day-to-day aspects of life, there are grids to stick to: those annoying blog posts which give you supposedly simple routines for cleaning your house, disciplining your children, making your own furniture, keeping all your plates spinning.

Often people are just trying to help. And yet often it's no help at all. It's a tyranny of expectations we can't meet, an image we can't keep up, relationships we can't find. Like the bloody lines on the wrapping paper, sometimes we want to scream, "*JUST LEAVE ME ALONE!*"

Advent is a time to be grateful for a Saviour who worked 'off-grid', rejecting the expectations of his day, and encouraging those around him to do likewise – not for the sake of being different, but for the sake of pursuing God's heart.

For example, he encouraged a rich man not to stick to the grid of investing his finances for himself – but to give them away and follow Jesus. (Matthew 19:16-22)

He encouraged His disciples not to stick to the grid of displaying their religion publicly – but to give, pray and fast in private. (Matthew 6:1-18)

He encouraged the Pharisees not to stick to the grid of judgement, stoning a woman to death because of her sexual sin – but rather to look at their own lives and confess their own sin. (John 8:1-11)

And the Bible encourages us to do the same today. Paul says:

Do not conform to the pattern of this world, but be transformed by the renewing of your mind. Then you will be able to test and approve what God's will is – his good, pleasing and perfect will.
(Romans 12:2)

This comes both as a challenge, and as a relief. Challenge, because there are things in this world that we *do* want to fit in with, grids which seem appealing and enjoyable – yet which we know are not what God desires for us. But also relief, because many of the grids of this world are suffocating or even damaging, and to be rid of them brings peace.

To give you two examples from my own life, I would like to conform to the worldly grid, or expectation, that a person my age, with my qualifications and earning potential, should own their own home – whereas I don't, and it's a regular challenge for me to trust God with our finances. But, as an example of where I am relieved not to have to meet the world's expectations, I can offer the grid of image and beauty: while I love to play with clothes and make-up, I know that my worth does not depend on how I look, because I was made by God and am already loved unconditionally by him.

- Which of the grids, or expectations, placed on you do you need to return to, and challenge? Ask God to reveal the areas where he wants you to conform to him, not the world.

- Are there things in your life which are stressful because you've become caught up in sticking to the grid? (They might overlap with your answers from yesterday.) Ask God to help you shift them.

Lord Jesus, thank you that your life here on earth was ground-shakingly revolutionary. Please allow me now to hear your voice as I ask you which parts of my life you want to shake up, perhaps an area of my life where I have moved forward unthinkingly, under the expectations of those around me, and not following your call. Help me to hear your voice, and adjust the direction I'm heading. Help me to know the peace and relief that following you brings. Amen.

Day 17: You Don't Always Get What You Want

At this stage in December, I'll typically have done most of my Christmas shopping, including gifts for our kids.

And at this stage in December, our kids will typically have produced brand new (and long) Christmas lists, which bear little or no resemblance to the lists they wrote last month, and from which I've been working.

It was a revelation one year, for example, to discover – mid-way through December – that my daughter wanted a camera. She hadn't thought of asking me, and she hadn't even written it on a list. She simply mentioned it in conversation, as if it was common knowledge.

Needless to say, I had to let her down gently, explaining that her presents had already been bought – as well as giving her a small lesson in the art of communication.

You don't always get what you want. *Sometimes you ask at the wrong time.*

My son is particularly ambitious when it comes to asking for things. When he ran out of his favourite snack, I showed him where the shopping list was kept, and told him that if he wrote down whatever we were running out of, I'd order it with our next shop – so he dutifully added 'banana chips' to the list.

But my boy isn't daft. Realising that whatever he wrote on the list seemed to magically appear in our house the following week, he tried his luck with 'hoverboard'.

You can't blame the boy for trying, can you? But, needless to say, I had to explain to him that he wouldn't be getting one. He couldn't expect such a large gift when it wasn't his birthday – and, anyway, I wasn't convinced that you could buy hoverboards from Morrisons.

You don't always get what you want. *Sometimes it's not appropriate.*

Sometimes we pray and pray and pray, and we don't get the response we want. Our lives are full of the imperfections, big and small, that we've been thinking about over the last couple of days, but we're just not seeing the breakthrough we'd like. This person didn't get healed. That person got made redundant. This difficult situation seems to have got worse, not better. It feels like God isn't there.

You don't always get what you want.

Sometimes, like my daughter, we get our timing wrong. God's timing is perfect, and ours is not. Perhaps we're asking for the right thing, but for some reason which we can't yet see, it will be a while before it's given to us.

Sometimes, like my son, we're asking for inappropriate things. We know that the Bible calls us again and again to seek the will of God, but we stray so far from our relationship with him, that the things we're asking for are not at all in keeping with his plan for us, our friends, or our family.

You don't always get what you want.

We know that our Father God *does* give good things to those who ask:

> *Which of you, if your son asks for bread, will give him a stone? Or if he asks for a fish, will give him a*

snake? If you, then, though you are evil, know how to give good gifts to your children, how much more will your Father in heaven give good gifts to those who ask him!"

(Matthew 7:9-11)

Yet we can all think of times when we asked for good things and didn't receive them. What's going on?

My husband and I have wisdom, or at least experience, that our children don't have. We don't give them everything they ask for, because we understand things that they don't. We can foresee the impact of a particular gift in a way that they can't quite yet.

God is infinitely wise and totally perfect – and we aren't. He gives only the right things at the right time. We can't understand why some things appear to be withheld – but, then again, we don't have God's perspective of the whole of humanity across the whole of time. One day, we will understand, but not now.

You don't always get what you want.

There's another aspect to this. My children probably know when they're being rather bold in their requests – but they still ask. They have a relationship with us which makes them entirely comfortable to approach us with confidence.

God wants us to approach him with confidence too. He wants us to ask. Maybe we won't get what we want, but he does want to hear our desires. What sort of Father doesn't want his children to speak to him, to ask for things, to rely on him?

> *Do not be anxious about anything, but in every situation, by prayer and petition, with thanksgiving, present your requests to God.*
> (Philippians 4:6)

Like my children – asking for what they want, but being able to trust the decision-making of their parents – we too need to hold in balance the boldness of asking God, with trust in his perfect will. My experience has often been that what God actually gives me (and the way he gives it) is far, far better than what I was hoping for when I made my original request!

You don't always get what you want – but your heavenly Father knows what is good, and gives it in abundance.

- Which of your prayers feels like it's going unanswered right now? Ask God for some encouragement to keep going, or some indication of why it may be the wrong thing at this time.

Dear Lord, I confess that sometimes I ask for the wrong things. But, worse than that, sometimes I don't ask at all. Give me a growing sense of confidence in you, so that, like a trusting child with a loving Father, I can freely approach you with everything that's causing me worry. And grow my love for you as God, rather than you as Giver, so that when some of my prayers go unanswered, my faith in you is not shaken, but strengthened, as I trust that your will is best for me. Amen.

DAY 18: YOU DON'T ALWAYS GET WHAT YOU DESERVE

Yesterday, we thought about the fact that we don't always get what we want.

But there's a lot going on in December about what we *deserve*, too. Santa only comes if you've been good. He only gives you what you deserve. The Elf on the Shelf watches your every move and only gives positive reports to Santa if you've been good. Adverts galore tell us to treat ourselves this Christmas – whether that be with food, drink, an expensive perfume or a romantic getaway – because we've worked hard this year and *we deserve it.*

I've been in shops with my kids during Advent, and some well-meaning stranger has said to them with a smile, "Have you been good? What's Santa bringing you?"

I never know how to respond, given that the kind lady (it's always a lady) hasn't asked for a theological conversation. I want to say that there's more to life than being 'good', and that good works don't always bring an immediate reward anyway. I want to say that my kids' presents come from us, not Santa – and we give because we love them, not because they've been good. But this, of course, is not what the lady signed up for, so I tend to laugh it off with a smile.

You see, the world is telling us that if we've been good, then we deserve a good reward. But God sees things differently. Far from telling us to be entitled and deserving, the Bible fixes our perspective on a God who is entitled to, and deserving of, everything we have and are. Why? Because, without him, we don't have life at all. Literally.

Jesus' encounter with two of his disciples, James and John, teaches us something of this:

> *Then James and John, the sons of Zebedee, came to him. "Teacher," they said, "we want you to do for us whatever we ask."*
>
> *"What do you want me to do for you?" he asked.*
>
> *They replied, "Let one of us sit at your right and the other at your left in your glory."*
>
> *"You don't know what you are asking," Jesus said. "Can you drink the cup I drink or be baptised with the baptism I am baptised with?"*

"We can," they answered.

Jesus said to them, "You will drink the cup I drink and be baptised with the baptism I am baptised with, but to sit at my right or left is not for me to grant. These places belong to those for whom they have been prepared."
(Mark 10:35-40)

It's easy to scoff at how arrogant James and John were being, but note that Jesus doesn't shoot them down before they begin. He *wants* to hear their request and he wants them to ask (see day 17). He wants us to ask as well.

And really, when we do ask God for things, are our attitudes much different to James and John's? How often do we feel God needs to give us something? That we deserve this or that because of all the time we spend serving God? How often do we storm ahead with our own plans for life, not giving a second thought to what God has planned for us?

The Bible goes further than this. What we *actually* deserve is summed up perfectly by Paul here:

For the wages of sin is death, but the gift of God is eternal life in Christ Jesus our Lord.
(Romans 6:23)

Did you catch that? What we *ultimately* deserve for our sin is death. That's big! Perhaps our good works aren't enough to change that.

But - you don't always get what you deserve.

And how wonderful for us that we don't! God doesn't want to give us death – he gave that to Jesus, who didn't deserve it. Instead of getting what *we* deserve, we get what *Jesus* deserves – life! Through Jesus' sacrifice, God has made each one of us as holy and acceptable to him as if we had never done anything wrong. It's not through our good works – which, however good, aren't good enough to keep us from death. It's through who Jesus was and what he did. How amazing is that?

- Are you willing to accept something you don't deserve?

- Can you get your head around the idea that you can't 'work' for God's gift, that it's entirely free?

Dear Jesus, through your birth came the best gift anyone has ever offered me: the gift of life, freedom from death, sin, guilt and condemnation. Thank you for taking the death I deserved. Embed this truth in me now, so that I may understand and embrace it more richly than I've ever done before. Amen.

REDEEMING OUR COMMUNITIES

DAY 19: THE GIVING OF AN UNNECESSARY GIFT

One of the things our family enjoys during December is making gifts for others.

I say 'family' – realistically it's just me, plus whichever kids are old enough to help and young enough to consider craft-with-Mum a great treat, and not a groan-inducing commitment which keeps one away from what one really wants to be doing (more often than not, gluing one's face to a screen).

It's become a tradition in our house because, a few years ago, I realised that several of my in-laws' friends insisted on being extremely generous to us at Christmas time. To begin with, I thought it was because we were newly-married, and therefore something of a novelty – but the gifts kept coming, and when our children arrived, the generosity continued to them.

I didn't exactly feel *obliged* to give something back – the friends in question certainly weren't giving in order to receive – but their gifts said something of what we meant to them, and I wanted to return the gesture by showing them how much they, their love and support, meant to us as a family too.

Knowing that there's not very much you can give someone older than sixty that they don't already have, or that they can't already afford to buy for themselves, I turned to the medium of homemade gifts, and they went down very well – surprisingly well. And, because it would appear that having coconut ice for breakfast on Boxing Day is a tradition which never gets boring, the gifts continue to go down well.

Homemade gifts abound at Christmas-time. Come December, even friends who never make *anything* through the year will be found scouring Pinterest and ordering cellophane bags and ribbons like there's about to be a national shortage.

We have been the recipients of some very special homemade gifts over the years – from the wonderfully scented Christmas play dough given to our son by his godmother, to the sloe gin given to me by a good friend before she went overseas for two months. I thought of her every time I had a glass.

I think going homemade is an appropriate way to celebrate Christmas, even if it's just the odd gift here or there. No one *needs* coconut ice, scented play dough or sloe gin – but each gift contains so much love, thought, energy and time, that it represents much more than just a foodstuff, or play material, or whatever it is.

Perhaps a homemade gift expresses what we struggle to put into words: that we value the ways in which this particular friend enriches our life through the year.

Jesus also received presents he didn't really *need*. There's a lot of rubbish out there in the newborn market, but even Mothercare, with its vast array of pointless baby products for neurotic parents, draws the line at gold, frankincense and myrrh.

These gifts, however, represented what the givers wanted to express to Jesus – in fact, they had a powerful prophetic quality.

Gold was given to recognise that Jesus was the promised new King, sent from God, born to man:

...They are all defying Caesar's decrees, saying that there is another king, one called Jesus.
(Acts 17:7)

Frankincense, which was used by priests, represented the role that Jesus would fulfil as the great High Priest: a completely new, and direct, way we could approach God, rather than the old ritual of going through a priest:

Therefore, since we have a great high priest who has ascended into heaven, Jesus the Son of God, let us hold firmly to the faith we profess. For we do not have a high priest who is unable to empathize with our weaknesses, but we have one who has been tempted in every way, just as we are – yet he did not sin. Let us then approach God's throne of grace with confidence, so that we may receive mercy and find grace to help us in our time of need.
(Hebrews 4:14-16)

And myrrh, a spice used to embalm a dead body, foretold Jesus' death – the means by which our sin could be dealt with forever:

But we do see Jesus, who was made lower than the angels for a little while, now crowned with glory and honour because he suffered death, so that by the grace of God he might taste death for everyone. (Hebrews 2:9)

None of these gifts were *needed* by Jesus – but each said something deeply significant about who he was.

- Which gifts are you giving this year which express gratitude for a relationship that has blessed you this year?

- Which of the three aspects of Jesus' character expressed by the wise men's gifts (King, High Priest, defeater of death) do you need to absorb more fully this Advent?

Lord Jesus, the wise men recognised that You were the promised King, the great High Priest, and one who would defeat death forever. I confess that I struggle to get my head around these concepts. Please embed them in me by your Holy Spirit, so that I may draw closer to you this Christmas. Amen.

DAY 20: WHEN THE LIGHT OF THE WORLD FEELS INSIGNIFICANT

For an otherwise laid-back soul, my husband is incredibly fussy about lighting. It's either too bright, or too dim, or placed in the wrong location, or facing the wrong direction.

There's a cul-de-sac not far from us where the residents totally cover their houses in amazing Christmas lights each year. Each year, the street welcomes thousands of visitors throughout Advent, and raise thousands of pounds for charity through a donations box.

Needless to say, my husband thinks it's ridiculous and tacky, and comes along begrudgingly, always outnumbered five to one in the decision to go and see these lights.

But I tend to think that if you can't enjoy a bit of tackiness at Christmas, when can you?

Besides, it's *totally* appropriate that we celebrate Christmas with lights – whether fairy lights, an Advent candle, or a full-blown rooftop Santa-in-a-helicopter – because, after all, we're celebrating the arrival of Jesus, *Light of the World.*

I wonder how clearly Jesus' light appears to be shining in your world right now. Perhaps you can see his light clearly in the joy of things going to plan this year. Perhaps even though you're going through a difficult period, you can still glimpse his light shining hope and peace in an otherwise tumultuous season of life.

Perhaps your life, or the life of someone you love, or the community around you, feels very dark right now. Loneliness, ill health, family pressures, debt, domestic violence, bereavement – not to mention the many terrible situations around the world which cause us anxiety – are just some of the darknesses which can feel stronger than the Light we're trying to celebrate.

But I want to suggest a way in which, however dark our world feels right now, we can still celebrate the Light of the World. Perhaps you don't feel so full of light this Christmas – and that's okay. But you can still cling to *hope:* a firm belief that, one day, Jesus' light will shine throughout the whole earth, and rid us of darkness forever.

However dark this year has been, or you're expecting Christmas to be, remember that Jesus *is* the Light of the World – whether that feels like a whole street of illuminated houses, or a tiny flickering flame – and that gives us hope to move forward in his strength.

Today, I give you something a bit different to mull over: an excerpt from *The Jesus Storybook Bible*, by Sally Lloyd-Jones, which was published in 2012. The passage is based on Luke 2. I think it explains what the Light of the World means in a fresh way:

> *...suddenly a bright new star appeared. Of all the stars in the dark vaulted heavens, this one shone clearer. It blazed in the night and made the other stars look pale beside it. God put it there when his baby Son was born – to be like a spotlight. Shining on him. Lighting up the darkness. Showing people the way to him...*

> *This baby would be like that bright star shining in the sky that night. A Light to light up the whole world. Chasing away darkness. Helping people to see. And the darker the night got, the brighter the star would shine.*

> (Jesus Storybook Bible, pages 184 and 190)

Whether life feels mostly light or mostly dark at the moment, commit yourself to clinging on to the hope that one day, Jesus' light will shine brighter than any darkness.

- Spend a few moments meditating on where Jesus, the Light of the World, is lighting up your life or your community. If everything feels dark, don't ignore this question! It's even more important in dark times to be able to see the Light who gives hope.

Dear Jesus, thank you that you are the Light of the World. Show me how you're lighting up the situations around me. And in dark times, help me to grasp the hope that even though things seem bad now, one day your light will shine so brightly that darkness will be eradicated forever. Amen.

If I'm ever asked for words to describe my identity, I usually come up with things like mum, wife, musician, cook or writer.

I don't tend to think of myself as a Vicar's Wife – *ever.* It's not deliberate – I was once a Vicar's Daughter, and I have absolutely no problem with being married to a vicar. In fact I quite like it. It's just that we were married before he became a vicar, and I did lots of things before that point, and I do lots of things now. I just kind of forget.

Except for one Christmas. It was a few years ago, and the Husband-Who's-A-Vicar was fairly new to his current job. I'd been roped in to play the organ at some service or other – possibly Christmas Day – and had popped along to the church building to practise. When I finished, I drove along the street to some of the tower blocks nearby, opened the car boot to reveal a rather lovely selection of hampers, and proceeded to knock on doors and give them out.

I chuckled inwardly, because this felt *very Vicar's-Wifely.* A spot of organ practice, followed by a

Christmas visit to the 'poor and needy' of the parish. Roll over, Charles Dickens.

I was distributing the hampers on behalf of a charity which gives out over a hundred in our city each year (and probably thousands nationally). Various groups and individuals from our church had contributed to these hampers, and it's now become a tradition for our house groups to make up a Christmas hamper each year.

The great thing about this charity is that it works with vulnerable people day in and day out. Charity is a long-term commitment: getting alongside others and walking with them through their difficulties, not chucking a few pounds in a charity box, or organising standing orders (although, realistically, these are helpful too!).

Our house group has made its hamper for the same family for several years running – it's a family we know from the school-gate, who have got a particularly rough deal in life. We know they are being supported through the year by this charity, and others associated with them.

In the Christmas story, we don't see 'charity', as such – we simply see a vulnerable family with an important job. We see a young, first-time mother, pregnant outside marriage, willing to face the scorn of others in order to obey her Lord. We see a perplexed father – who isn't *actually* the father, but has the humility to adopt a son who doesn't share his genes, and raise him as if he did. And we see a tiny baby, who is at risk of being killed by a jealous political ruler.

If the Christmas story means anything to us, let's not judge why or how others are in the situations they're in – but instead learn to walk alongside them, helping and being helped, befriending, learning from each other's stories. Yesterday, we thought about times in our lives when the Light of the World doesn't feel so bright. Perhaps God is calling us to bring his light into the lives of those around us, whose situations feel dark and hopeless right now.

Whoever wants to become great among you must be your servant...whoever wants to be first must be your slave – just as the Son of Man did not come to be served, but to serve, and to give his life as a ransom for many. (Matthew 20:26-28)

The mere idea of supporting others can seem exhausting when we're already shattered by the other demands of life. But what if God wasn't calling us to heal the world, but simply serve in the opportunities he provides? For sure, it will involve sacrifice, and it may feel overwhelming at times, but it shouldn't feel unmanageable. By taking small steps to serve the people God has put in our lives, we can trust him to fill the gaps we can't.

- Which **one** person in your life will you commit to walking alongside in the coming year? (This might be someone who is 'poor' financially, socially, physically or mentally – someone you can help.)

Father God, you deliberately sent your Son into a vulnerable situation, and I praise you for what this teaches me about your heart for the poor. Thank you that you love all who you have made. Help me to make time in the coming year for whoever you've put in my life to walk alongside. Amen.

Day 22: The Vicar's Kid at Christmas

Vicarages are crazy places at Christmas. I should know – I've been a vicar's daughter, and I am now a vicar's wife.

Every time you try to tidy up for the next get-together, the house becomes flooded with boxes of Christmas flyers, or bags of food for a community Christmas lunch.

But vicarages are also fun places at Christmas. I don't know if it was my frugal parents, or the fact it was the 1980s (probably a bit of both), but when I was a kid, we didn't tend to see a box of chocolates all year, so the appearance of several tins of Roses and Quality Street at Christmas from grateful parishioners, in addition to posh cheese boards and smoked salmon, got me excited just a little.

These days, we still receive generous gifts from our church family, and I'm particularly in awe of those who've made time to buy and wrap a gift for *each* of our children. I mean – we have quite a few, so that's a tall order. It's not at all expected – a tub of Heroes would be more than appreciated by the six of us together. But there are some at our church who are *particularly* good at looking out for our children, and we appreciate it so much.

Being a vicar's kid can be wonderful, but it can also be pretty tough. Your ordained parent has to work funny hours. You have to share your home – and your life – with any odds and sods your parent brings home (and some of them are *very* odd). You're fending for yourself at church each week, because both of your parents are otherwise engaged (very rarely does a vicar's spouse get off scot-free on a Sunday).

The gifts received by our kids are a way of saying, "Thank you for lending us your Dad. We see you, and are so grateful for what you give up in order for us to be blessed by his leadership."

I think there's a message here about seeing the unseen. Yesterday we thought about those who God is calling us to invest more time in. Perhaps the person you thought of is 'unseen' by others.

Some of our church family are great at seeing our kids – not just buying them lovely Christmas presents, but making time for them throughout the year. Others in our church are great at seeing the single mums, or the older folk, or those recently bereaved or divorced. We all have different gifts, and we all 'see' different people at different times and for different reasons.

I don't need to remind you that Jesus 'saw' the unseen – encounters with prostitutes and tax collectors are strewn through the gospels like over-keen confetti. But sometimes we forget that there were a heck of a lot of people that Jesus *didn't* minister to, as well. It wasn't that they'd been left out of the Kingdom of Heaven – but that it was going to be down to someone else to share the good news with them. Jesus came primarily for the Jewish people – it was Peter, and later Paul, who would have a ministry among the Gentiles.

The story of Jesus healing the daughter of a Canaanite woman is really striking. It does seem as if Jesus isn't going to act, purely because the woman isn't a Jew. In the end he does, because her strong faith is so evident:

Leaving that place, Jesus withdrew to the region of Tyre and Sidon. A Canaanite woman from that vicinity came to him, crying out, "Lord, Son of David, have mercy on me! My daughter is demon-possessed and suffering terribly."

Jesus did not answer a word. So his disciples came to him and urged him, "Send her away, for she keeps crying out after us."

He answered, "I was sent only to the lost sheep of Israel."

The woman came and knelt before him. "Lord, help me!" she said.

He replied, "It is not right to take the children's bread and toss it to the dogs."

"Yes it is, Lord," she said. "Even the dogs eat the crumbs that fall from their master's table."

Then Jesus said to her, "Woman, you have great faith! Your request is granted." And her daughter was healed at that moment.
(Matthew 15:21-28)

Although Jesus *does* heal the girl, he makes it quite clear that he has come for the Israelites – not the Canaanites. And of course the gospel accounts only tell who he *did* minister to – we're left to fill in the gaps of all those he wouldn't have been able to engage with, through lack of time or opportunity.

I'm very grateful for those in our church family who see our kids. I'm also delighted by those who pour their gifts and time into *different* people who need encouragement. Where would we be if everyone spoilt our kids at Christmas, but never invited the single parents for Christmas lunch? Or if all the single parents were well cared-for, but the elderly or housebound were never visited? The body of Christ works best when we look out for each other.

- Who are the unseen people in your life; those who need an encouraging card written to them, or a small gift, or day-by-day messages of support? Don't try to 'see' everyone, but allow God to bring to mind a person or two he wants you to encourage over the next few months.

Dear Father God, you see everyone. No one is left out of your invitation to the Kingdom of Heaven. Thank you for your hospitality. And thank you that you use us as your 'eyes', to notice and walk beside those who need encouragement. Please tell me who you would like me to draw alongside during this coming year. Amen.

DAY 23: THE JOBS LEFT UNDONE

We're on the home run now, folks. Whether Christmas Day is being anticipated with excitement, or with rising levels of stress, it will be here (and over) soon.

I expect you're ticking off the jobs at quite a pace. Ordering food. Buying and wrapping gifts. Making sure you have enough airbeds and pillows for those staying with you.

However, perhaps there are also jobs you haven't done, or won't get a chance to do. The DIY jobs you'd wanted to complete in time for your family to arrive will now not happen. Tasks you'd hoped to finish at work have been shelved for January. Time is running out, and it's a case of taking short-cuts, or leaving things out altogether.

That's always the case for me. The more I tick off my list, the more seems to be added. The hopes I had of making some puddings ahead of a big family gathering may have to be whittled down to ordering a few ready-made cheesecakes. I almost certainly won't have started packing for our trip to see the in-laws. And you can bet your bottom dollar that none of the food I've contributed to my children's Christmas parties will have been homemade.

There's something good about high expectations: they keep us motivated, aiming for our best. But perhaps they sometimes have the opposite effect: *de-motivating* us. Fuelling the little voice inside my head which says, *"You've failed. You haven't met your expectations. You haven't kept all the plates spinning. You're a mess."*

Whenever I don't manage to do things I was hoping to do, I have to stop and tell myself, *"But you weren't called to do that. You have four children. You have adoption clouding the mix. You have a husband with a pastorally-demanding job. You're not called to have a show-home/cook everything from scratch/commit to this voluntary body or that community group."* (Insert whatever is most appropriate for you into the last sentence.)

It's an enormous comfort to me to realise that we each have different callings. I may be blessed by entering someone else's immaculate house – but they may be blessed by my messy parenting. I may be blessed by the financial giving of someone on a great salary – but they may be blessed by my heart for adoption.

We are not called to do *everything*, much as it's hard for some of us to accept this. Mary had a very clear sense of calling, and she did it with obedience and joy.

> *And Mary said:*
> *"My soul glorifies the Lord*
> *and my spirit rejoices in God my Saviour,*
> *for he has been mindful*
> *of the humble state of his servant.*
> *From now on all generations will call me blessed,*
> *for the Mighty One has done great things for me -*
> *holy is his name.*
> (Luke 1:46-49)

We can all learn from Mary's attitude. What has God called us to do? Can we honestly say that our souls 'glorify the Lord' for giving us this calling, whether it's a job, a vocation, a lifestyle choice or anything else? Can we, like Mary, genuinely call ourselves 'blessed'? And do others describe us that way? Or do we have such a frenetic pace of life, trying to be all things to all people, that no-one would ever in a million years describe our lives as 'blessed'?

When we are distracted by callings which are not ours, we can remember Mary's clear sense of calling and her joyous response to the knowledge that God wanted to use her in his plans. Perhaps we need to adopt a discipline of reminding ourselves not to get down-hearted when we fail to achieve things which God hasn't called us to in the first place.

- Do you get tempted to take on too much, or to do what you're already doing to impossibly high standards?

- As the coming year draws closer, what is your actual calling, and what distracts you from it? How will you pursue it next year?

Lord God, thank you that you have planned good works for me to do (Ephesians 2:10), and thank you that you have planned **other** good works for **other** people to do. As I end this year and look towards the next, please give me a clearer sense of calling, so that I may pursue what you have asked of me with the same obedience and joy that Mary did. Help me not to compare myself with others who have been given different callings. Amen.

Day 24: Cheerleaders

The big day is nearly here! How are you feeling? Stressed, like there's still so much to do? Or relaxed, because it's all done?

If you've made it this far, please give yourself a hearty pat on the back. You've made it further than I ever did with any Advent devotional I tried to read. Like I said in my introduction, this book started life as a series of blog posts I wrote in December 2017 to try and help me stay spiritually focused throughout Advent. If I've helped you to do the same, then all glory to God.

To be honest, on December 24th 2017, I was giving myself a pat on the back too. The fact I'd just written 24 devotionals was mind-boggling – I never thought I'd make it to the end either!

The biggest reason that I managed it was the encouragement I'd received throughout the month. December is a busy month for all of us, so the fact that some wonderful people had taken a few minutes out of their busy lives to send me comments, texts, messages or emails, and spur me on, meant the world to me.

We all need cheerleaders, right? People who can congratulate us when things are going well, pick us up when they're not, and give us a good old talking-to when we're allowing negative thoughts to stop us from taking positive action.

Hebrews 12 likens the journey of faith to a race:

> *Therefore, since we are surrounded by such a great cloud of witnesses, let us throw off everything that hinders and the sin that so easily entangles. And let us run with perseverance the race marked out for us, fixing our eyes on Jesus, the pioneer and perfecter of faith. For the joy set before him he endured the cross, scorning its shame, and sat down at the right hand of the throne of God. Consider him who endured such opposition from sinners, so that you will not grow weary and lose heart.*
> (Hebrews 12:1-3)

Advent is a small representation of the journey that we're all on – the journey to draw closer to that babe in the manger, and this passage in Hebrews describes this journey as a race.

Think about that for a minute. No one runs an actual race without support from the sidelines. Whether it's the London Marathon, or a school sports day, the idea that any of us would run a race without others cheering us on is faintly ridiculous. Listen to any sportsperson after winning a race, match or game, and they will inevitably mention the support of the crowd as a crucial factor in their success.

Our Christian 'race' can sometimes feel as easy as pie. Sometimes it's a joy, sometimes it takes courage, sometimes it feels like climbing a wall with no support. On occasions it's the last thing we want to do, and on others it's the only thing we're able to do. But we can't do it without one another.

There are two other things I'd like to draw out from this passage in Hebrews. Firstly, when our Christian journey feels tough, we are meant to remember Jesus, who endured the cross and 'opposition from sinners'. There is nothing we will go through that will be tougher than that. Jesus went through this for the joy of being with God forever – and one day, after this tough race has finished, we will know that joy as well.

Secondly, we are told to 'throw off everything that hinders and the sin that so easily entangles'. It would be ludicrous for a marathon-runner to carry a backpack or wear a heavy overcoat, but we are just as ludicrous when we try to run our spiritual race whilst carrying burdens that Jesus wants to take from us. So often, we are loath to look at our own lives and deal with the sin we find, even though we know, deep down, that to do so will allow us to move forward in our relationship with Jesus.

When we are struggling, it is not always as a direct result of our sin, of course, but I know that in my own life, it so often is. I want the blessings of a close relationship with God, a sense of his calling in my life, the joy and the peace that come from knowing him – and yet I stubbornly refuse to deal with a sinful attitude, a grudge against a friend, or the ungodly way I interact with my children. Like a heavy overcoat worn by a marathon runner, this is going to significantly hinder my chances of reaching the end point well.

- However easy or difficult your Christian journey feels right now, allow God to speak into one area where he wants to offer encouragement, comfort, or challenge. You could ask, "Lord, where do you want me to grow right now?

- Who are the cheerleaders in your life right now? Why not send them a quick text to thank them for their friendship and support this year? (I'd say write a letter, but this is December 24th and I'm not that stupid. But, if you felt so moved, it could be something you plan to do in January.)

Lord God, thank you for your precious gift of Jesus. Thank you that, through his faithful endurance of the race you'd set out for him, I can not only have eternal life with you, but also a friend who empathises with my own suffering. Thank you for the cheerleaders you have put in my life who spur me on to complete my race. Please equip me to encourage others around me, so that we may all enjoy the crown of eternal life when our race ends. Amen.

Thank you so much for journeying with me this Advent. I pray God has used these devotions to keep you sane during December, and to help you reflect over the last year and anticipate the next one with joy and excitement. Above all, I hope you're a little closer to, and more excited to serve, the God who sent his Son to save us, and will send him again to claim us for heaven.

I'd love to stay in touch and hear how you've used this book. You can follow me on Facebook (Desertmum), Twitter (@DesertMumBlog) or Instagram (@desertmumblog). If you've enjoyed this book, you might enjoy my blog, where I write on faith, family, adoption, discipleship, chocolate, and anything else that takes my fancy – you can find it at lucyrycroft.com

A very, very blessed Christmas to you and those around you!